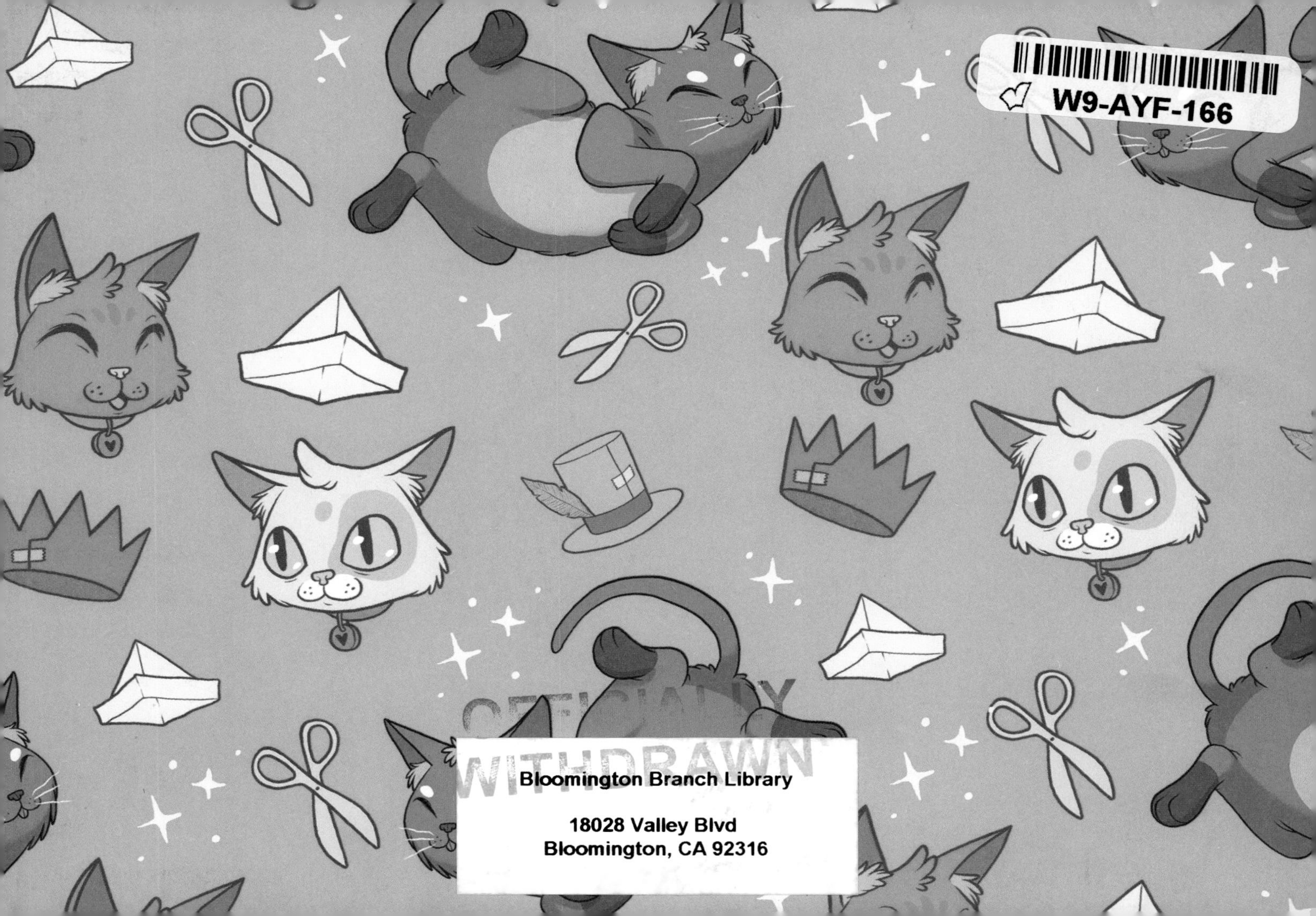

ALSO BY ADAM ELLIS

Books of Adam: The Blunder Years

TINY HATS ON CATS

BECAUSE EVERY CAT
DESERVES TO FEEL FANCY

ADAM ELLIS

GRAND CENTRAL
PUBLISHING

NEW YORK · BOSTON

Grand Central Publishing
Hachette Book Group
1290 Avenue of the Americas
New York, NY 10104
www.HachetteBookGroup.com
Printed in the United States of America
Q—MA

First Edition: October 2015

10 9 8 7 6 5 4 3 2 1

Grand Central Publishing is a division of Hachette Book Group, Inc.

The Grand Central Publishing name and logo is a trademark of
Hachette Book Group, Inc.

The Hachette Speakers Bureau provides a wide range of authors for speaking events.
To find out more, go to www.hachettespeakersbureau.com or call (866) 376-6591.

The publisher is not responsible for websites (or their content)
that are not owned by the publisher.

LIBRARY OF CONGRESS CATALOGING-IN-PUBLICATION DATA
Ellis, Adam.
Tiny hats on cats : because every cat deserves to feel fancy / Adam Ellis.
pages cm
ISBN 978-1-4555-5813-1 (hardback) — ISBN 978-1-4555-5812-4 (ebook) 1. Paper hat making. 2. Cats—
Pictorial works. I. Title.
TT870.E454 2015
745.59—dc23
2015025990

This book is dedicated to my two cats,

MAXWELL AND PEPPERCORN.

Thank you for being so patient.
You both deserve treats.

CONTENTS

INTRODUCTION

Maxwell was dirty and terrified when I first met him, hunched in the corner of his kennel cage at the animal shelter, his eyes wide with alarm. I'd brought my black cat Peppercorn in for a checkup, and while she was with the vet I decided to check out the available cats in the showroom. I'd been thinking about getting a second kitten for Peppercorn to play with. I noticed Maxwell, trying in vain to make himself as small as possible behind his food dish.

I asked about him, and when the shelter worker brought him out I noticed he was missing one of his front legs. Several black stitches poked out of the nub that remained. "He came in yesterday with a paralyzed leg, so we had to chop it off," the worker told me matter-of-factly. "We're not sure how he lost it. You're actually the first person to ask to hold him all day. People see he's missing a limb and move on to other cats. We're sort of worried about him."

Every muscle in Maxwell's body was tense as I held him, like a scared rabbit. He gazed around the room nervously, but he didn't struggle to get away. I petted him awhile, and after a few minutes he relaxed, even starting to purr in my arms. When he looked up at me with his big Disney eyes, I knew I was going to be taking him home with me.

He spent the better part of two weeks hiding under my bed, only venturing out when he heard the sound of a sardine can opening. But eventually, little by little, he started to cautiously explore my bedroom, then the living room, and finally the kitchen. It took a couple of months before he was really comfortable in his new home, but now he's the sweetest, most affectionate cat I've ever met. He's actually a little too comfortable, if you ask me. I might make him get a job soon, but I digress.

In addition to being a sweetheart, Maxwell is also incredibly patient. When I found some old leftover construction paper and decided it would be funny to make him a paper top hat, he actually sat still when I put it on his head and took a photo. I put it on Instagram and it was surprisingly popular, so I decided to make a few more. Before I knew it I had more than a hundred paper hats crowding my mantel and Maxwell had a healthy following online. *Tiny Hats on Cats* was born.

This book is the amalgamation of the Tiny Hats project. I couldn't have done it without the help of Maxwell (and Pepper, even though she's never been as patient with hats—she'd rather eat them than wear them, but I can occasionally convince her to cooperate with treats).

Enjoy!

HATS ON CATS

Army Cap

Boonie Hat

Bowler Hat

Chef Hat

Conquistador Helmet

Cowboy Hat

Crown

Fedora

Golf Cap

Gondolier Hat

Graduation Cap

Holiday Hat

Knight's Helmet

Mad Hatter Hat

Marching Band Hat

Military Captain Hat

Party Hat

Pilgrim Hat

Pirate Hat

Pope Hat

Princess Cone

Propeller Hat

Robin Hood Hat

Safari Helmet

Sailor Hat

Samurai Helmet (Kabuto)

Sandwich Hat

Service Hat

Sherlock Hat

Snapback

Summer Hat

Tam-o-Shanter

Top Hat

Tricorn

Valkyrie Hat

Witch Hat

INSTRUCTIONS

AFFIXING A HAT TO YOUR CAT

If your cat is calm and relaxed, you can probably rest the hat on her head and snap a couple of quick photos for Instagram before she moves. If you're having trouble with the hat sliding off, a small square of double-stick tape will do the trick! It's not sticky enough harm your feline friend, and you'll be able to get some more dramatic angles during fashion shoots.

My general rule when working with animals is the same as the Humane Society's: don't do anything to an animal you wouldn't do to a newborn baby. I personally have no problem taping things to infants, but perhaps not everyone feels the same. It's up to you.

TOOLS YOU'LL NEED

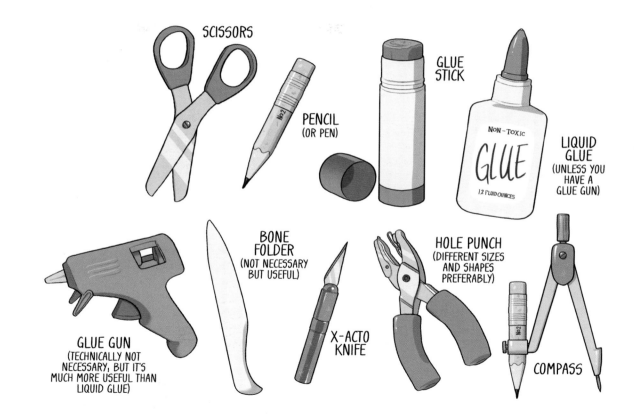

SCISSORS

PENCIL (OR PEN)

GLUE STICK

NON-TOXIC GLUE 12 FLUID OUNCES

LIQUID GLUE (UNLESS YOU HAVE A GLUE GUN)

GLUE GUN (TECHNICALLY NOT NECESSARY, BUT IT'S MUCH MORE USEFUL THAN LIQUID GLUE)

BONE FOLDER (NOT NECESSARY BUT USEFUL)

X-ACTO KNIFE

HOLE PUNCH (DIFFERENT SIZES AND SHAPES PREFERABLY)

COMPASS

THE BASICS

BASIC CYLINDERS

1. Cut out a rectangular shape of paper.

2. Curl it around your finger or a pencil and glue it into a tube. Experiment with size and shape to make shorter and taller hats.

DOMES

1. To make a dome, you first need a template. Refer to page 49
   for dome templates and choose one for your dome.

2. Using your template, trace six arches along the edge of your paper. Each arch should touch.

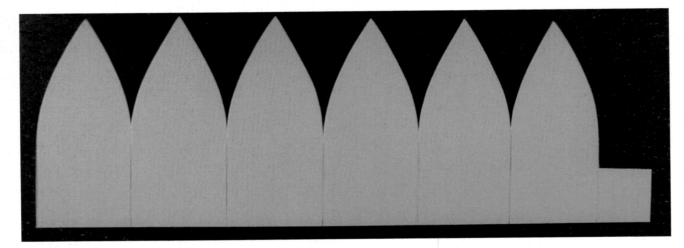

3. Cut out the arches as shown, leaving a flap at one end.

4. Curl this piece around into a sort of crown shape and use the flap to glue it.

5. Curl the points of the arches in slightly. Cut out a small circle of paper and glue it behind one of the arch points.

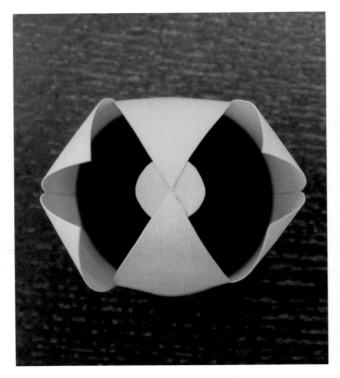 

6. Glue the opposite arch point to the paper circle, making sure the arches touch in the center.

7. Glue two more opposing arches to the circle in the center.

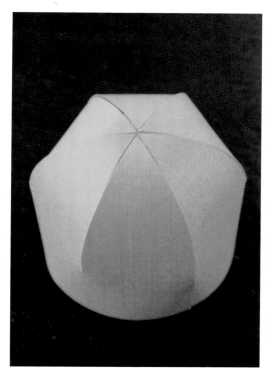

8. Glue down the remaining arches.

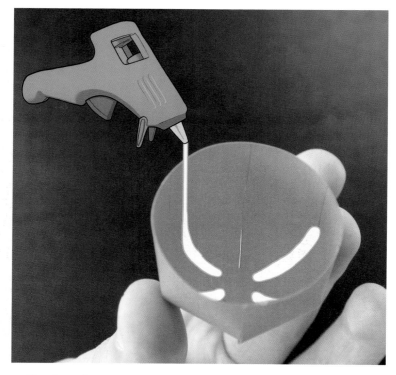

9. Use hot glue to seal the inner seams of the dome.

GLUING SHAPES ONTO PAPER BASES

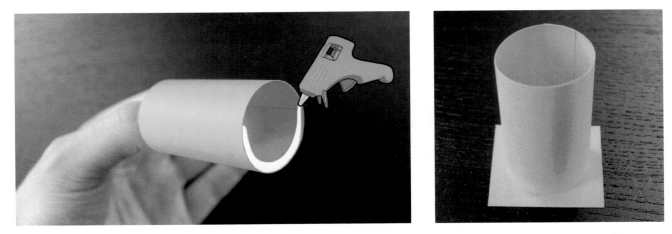

1. When you have a shape you need to glue to a base, use your hot glue gun to drizzle a line of glue just inside the shape. It's okay to use a liberal amount; just make sure it's not over-flowing from the shape.

2. Rest the shape on its paper base. Either hold it down with your hands or use a paperweight. The hot glue inside will drizzle down and seal the inside edge. Make sure to bring the paper pieces together while the glue is still warm, or else it won't seal properly. Now you can trim the excess of the base around the shape you just glued to it. This can take a little bit of practice, but it's easy once you get the hang of it!

DOME TEMPLATES

FOR EACH OF THE HATS IN THIS BOOK, I USED TEMPLATE 2.
OTHER TEMPLATES CAN BE SUBSTITUTED IF YOUR CAT'S HEAD
IS ON THE SMALLER OR LARGER SIDE, BUT KEEP IN MIND THAT
OTHER MEASUREMENTS WILL NEED TO BE SIMILARLY ADJUSTED.

TO USE THESE TEMPLATES, TRACE THEM WITH A SHEET OF
PAPER AND CAREFULLY CUT THEM OUT.

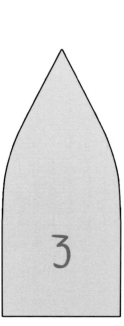

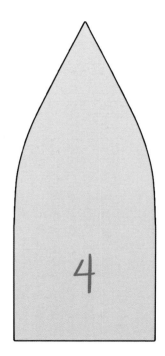

THE ACCESSORIES

BOW

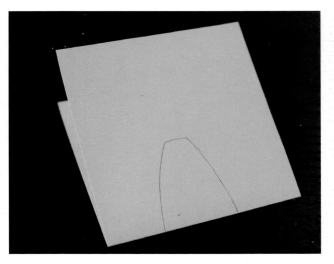

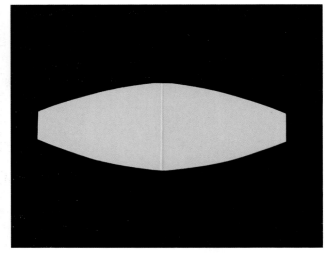

1. Fold a piece of paper in half and draw a shape like the one shown—sort of a tall trapezoid with curved sides.

2. Cut out the shape and unfold it. This is your bow template. You can make many of these in all different sizes if you want.

3. Fold another piece of paper, and line up the bow template against the folded edge lengthwise. Either trace around the template, or cut around it carefully.

4. Cut out and unfold this long piece.

5. If your paper has a pattern, make sure it's facing downward, then curl the sides of the paper inward and glue each end to the middle of the piece. It should line up perfectly.

6. Cut a long, thin strip of paper, at least several inches long.

7. Wrap this strip around the center of your bow shape, making at least several passes around it. Stop once the center of the bow has a thickness to your liking, then glue it and trim the excess.

8. Glue two short strips behind the bow, trim them to look like ribbon, and you're done!

FEATHERS AND LEAVES

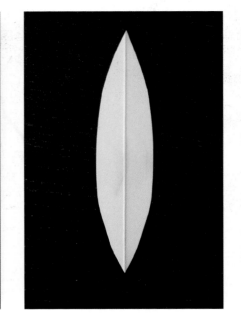

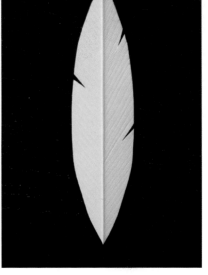

1. Fold a piece of paper in half.

2. Cut an oblong curve along the fold, then open the piece of paper.

3. Cut little notches into the sides of the feather shape. For leaves, just make a shorter, wider feather shape.

LILY

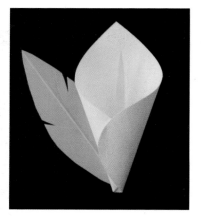

1. Cut a fat raindrop shape out of a piece of paper.

2. Curl the edges of the paper.

3. Glue the base into a cone shape, overlapping one side on the other.

4. Glue a sliver of paper into the middle of the cone, and add a green leaf behind the lily.

ROSE

1. Cut six squares.

2. Take one square and fold it in half.

3. Fold it in half again.

4. Make sure the part with four edges is pointing upward, and fold one edge about halfway across the square.

5. Fold the other edge in the same manner, but in the opposite direction.

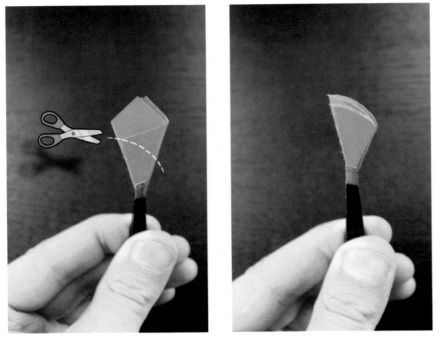 

6. Make a curved cut across the folded piece as shown.

7. Unfold the piece, and you should have a flower shape. Follow steps 2—7 for the remaining paper squares.

8. Trim your six flower shapes as shown.

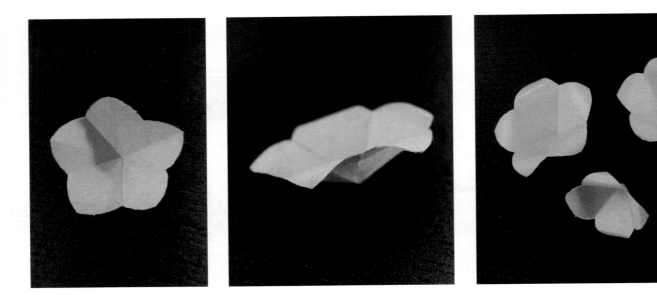

9. Take your largest flower piece, and glue it together over the gap you cut out.

10. Curl the petals of this flower shape downward.

11. Repeat these steps with the next three largest flower pieces.

 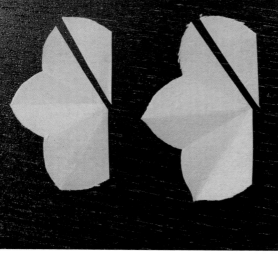 

12. Take one of the flower shapes you cut in half and glue each of the two halves into a cone. Since these don't have an extra half petal to use as a glue flap, just overlap one petal across another slightly.

13. Take the other two half-flower shapes and trim an extra half petal off them.

14. Discard the pieces you trimmed off, and glue the larger pieces into a two-petal cone.

15. Take your two largest flower pieces, and glue one into the other as shown.

16. Keep gluing flower shapes into the

center of the rose, descending by size.

17. Cut an angular shape like the one pictured.

18. Roll it up lengthwise and glue it into the very center of the rose. This doesn't have to be perfect and you can trim it to be shorter.

THE HATS

ARMY CAP

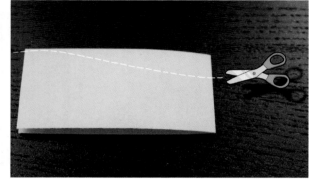

1. Cut a strip of paper about 6 inches long and 1 inch wide, depending on how big your cat's head is.

2. Fold the strip of paper in half, and make a wavy cut along the top as shown. Make sure you start the cut where the paper fold is.

3. Open the paper. It should look like the rolling hills of Tuscany.

4. Curl and glue the paper into a cylinder shape.

5. The slanted side of the cylinder is going to be the top of your hat. Glue it down to a piece of paper of the same color, then trim the excess once it's dry.

6. Now for the brim. Glue the hat onto a rectangular piece of paper, leaving enough room in the front of the hat to cut the shape of the brim.

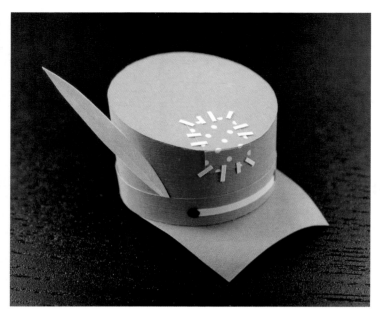

7. Once the glue is dry, trim around the hat. Leave a section jutting out in the front.

8. Curl the corners of the brim, and add whatever details you desire. I added a small strip of paper in the front, and used a small hole punch to make a button on each side. The patch was made with patterned scrapbook paper and tiny strips of white paper for the stitching.

BOONIE HAT

3. Flip the sides and glue them to the body of the hat. Cut two small circles (or use a hole punch) and glue them to either side of where the flaps meet the hat. Add details like feathers or flowers.

1. Make a short cylinder, and glue it down to a piece of paper of the same color or pattern. Trim once it's dry, then glue a thin band of contrasting paper around the base of the hat.

2. Using your compass, cut a circle that is roughly ¾ inch larger all around than the base of your hat. This doesn't have to be exact. Glue the cylinder down.

BOWLER
HAT

1. Start by creating a dome, then measure out a strip of contrasting paper and glue it around the base.

2. Use your protractor to cut a circle that extends roughly ⅓ inch beyond the base of your dome. Glue down the dome.

3. Once the hat is dry, curl up the edges on either side. Add whatever details your heart desires.

CHEF HAT

1. Cut a square of paper roughly 5 inches wide and long. Draw a line across the paper about 1½ inches up from the bottom, and another one about ⅓ inch down from the top.

2. Make a series of cuts between the two lines you've just drawn. These cuts should extend from one line to the other, and be spaced about ¼ inch from each other. Your series of cuts should go all the way across the paper.

3. After making these cuts, slice off one of the strips including the top portion and discard it. The bit you leave on the bottom portion will end up being your glue flap when you fold this hat into a cylinder, but let's not get ahead of ourselves.

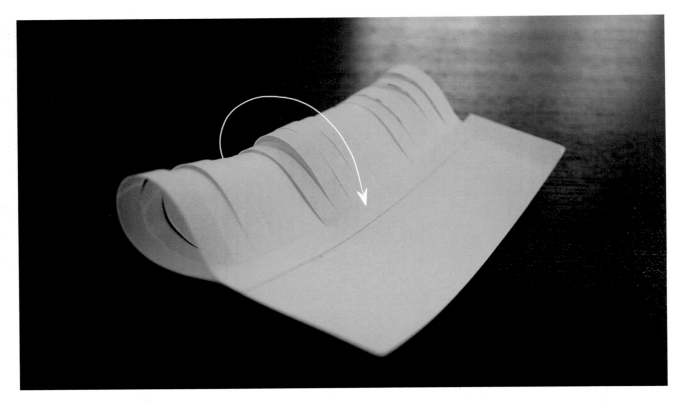

4. Curl the top part of your paper and glue it down to the bottom part. Make sure the lines you drew are facing inward. Even though you can't see the lines, do your best to make sure they meet.

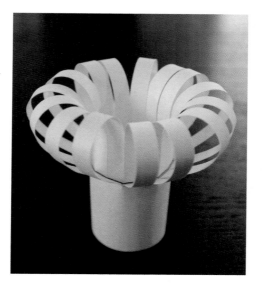

5. Once everything is dry, gently curl the whole hat into a cylinder, then use the flap you cut in step 3 to glue the hat together. The curly strands on top will probably need to be rearranged and bent outward a bit.

6. Add a decorative band around the base of the poufy top, then add a bow.

CONQUISTADOR
HELMET

1. Cut a dome template, but don't fold it into a dome shape yet.

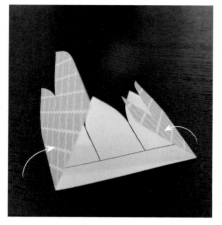

2. Flip the template over, so the side you drew on is facing up. Fold two arches in on one side; on the other side, fold one arch and the glue flap in.

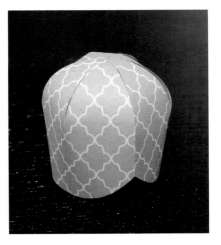

3. Trim the edges off the bottom corners as shown, making sure the edges are curved.

4. Unfold the paper, then continue with the normal directions for making a dome.

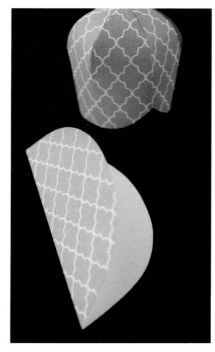

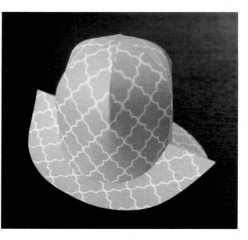

. . . Make sure the fold of the circular shape fits into the indentations of the dome.

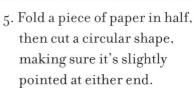

5. Fold a piece of paper in half, then cut a circular shape, making sure it's slightly pointed at either end.

6. Fold the circle back in half, then glue it underneath the base of the dome.

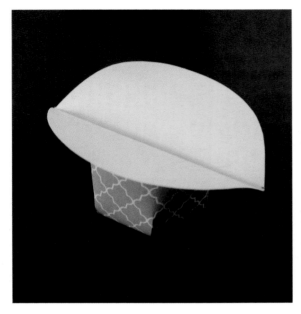

. . . This is more easily done if you glue the base down to one side of the dome's base then, once it's dry, glue the other side.

7. Fold a new piece of paper in half and cut it into a long feather shape. It should be roughly 4–5 inches long, but there might be some trial and error involved.

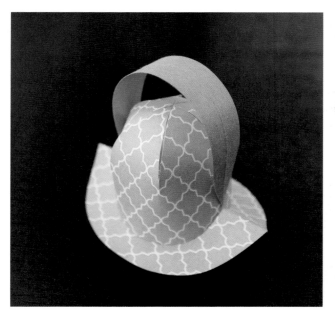

8. Glue the feather shape to the top of the helmet, starting from the front and arcing toward the back.

9. Add details like feather and flowers.

COWBOY HAT

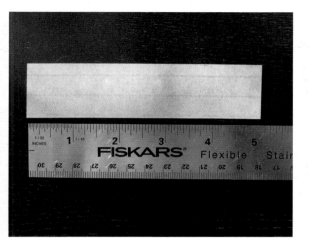

1. Cut a strip of paper about 5 inches long and 1 inch wide.

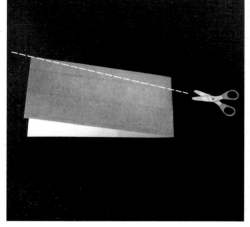

2. Fold the paper in half lengthwise.

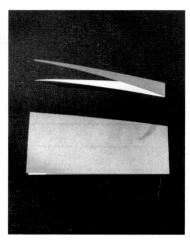

3. Make a diagonal cut across the top of the folded paper as shown.

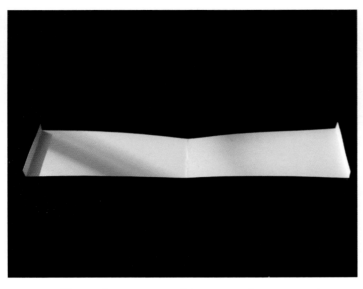

4. Open the paper, making sure the pattern is facing down (if there's no pattern, it doesn't matter). Fold each end up.

5. Fold the entire strip into a circular shape, gluing the two folded pieces together. Make sure the pattern is facing outward, and the folded pieces are glued together inward.

6. Glue a thin strip of contrasting paper around the flat base of the hat, then cut a small square of paper big enough to cover the top of the hat.

7. Flip the hat over and glue it down to the piece of paper you just cut. This is most easily done by dabbing the top of the hat with a glue stick, pressing it down onto the square piece of paper, then reinforcing the inner seams with a glue gun.

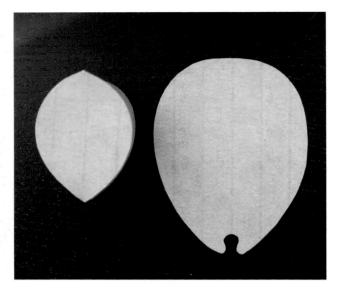

8. Once the hat is totally dry, trim the edges.

9. Cut out an egg-shaped piece of paper. You can eyeball the size by placing the hat on a sheet of paper and making a rough trace around it, about ½ inch outside the base of the hat. Then cut a small circular shape into the front of the hat as shown. You can use a hole punch for this if you want, or leave the egg-shaped piece intact if that's what your heart desires.

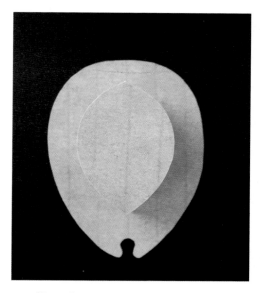

10. Glue the hat onto the base.

11. Curl up the sides of the hat and add whatever details you want.

CROWN

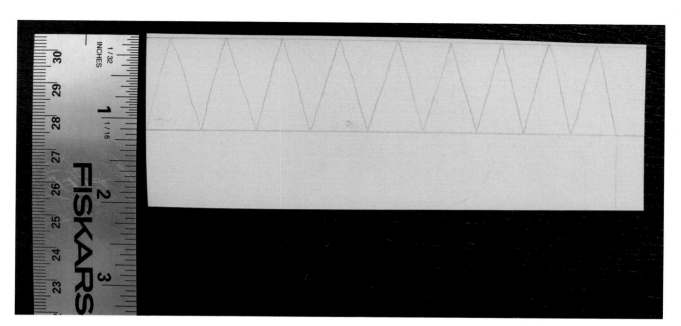

1. Cut a strip of paper roughly 5–6 inches long, depending on the size of your cat's head. It should be about 2 inches wide, but you can adjust the width if you want a taller or shorter crown. Measure a line across the paper lengthwise, then draw a series of diagonal triangle shapes.

Make sure you leave a glue flap at one end of the paper. None of this has to be exact, since crowns can vary in appearance. If you want, you can glue this strip of paper to a patterned paper of the same size, so your crown will have a unique interior, as you can see in later steps.

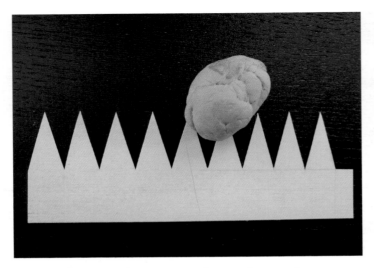

2. Cut away the top triangles as shown, then erase your pencil marks.

3. This step is optional, but it's an added visual element. Use a hole punch at the base of the crown's points.

4. Glue the paper into a cylinder shape. Look at that crown! Good job.

5. Add a decorative band around the base. To make "jewels," drop tiny globs of glue from your glue gun onto colored construction paper. Once dry, carefully peel them off and glue them onto your crown.

FEDORA

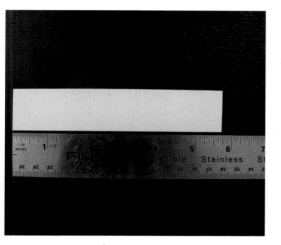

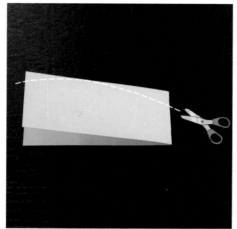

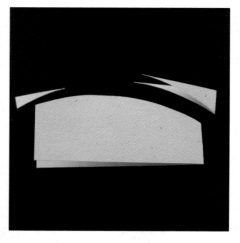

1. Cut a strip of paper 1 inch wide and a little under 6 inches in length.

2. Fold the paper in half lengthwise.

3. Make a curved cut along the top as shown. The cut should start where the fold is, and should start lower than where the cut ends.

4. Open the paper, and fold the edges up into glue flaps.

5. Curl the paper around into an oblong circular shape, and glue the flaps together, making sure they point inward.

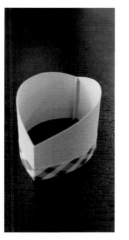

6. Glue a thin, decorative band around the base.

7. Cut a rectangular shape large enough to cover the top of the hat, and fold it in half hot-dog-style. Take a break and eat an actual hot dog if you wish.

8. You're going to glue this triangle onto the top of the hat. It's easiest if you flip the hat over and glue it down to the paper as shown. You can use your bone folder to curl the rectangular piece of paper a bit, and that way the hat will fit more easily. Dab the top of the hat with a glue stick, then press it down to the rectangle. Once it's dry, reinforce the inside seams with hot glue.

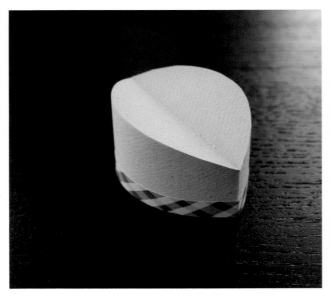

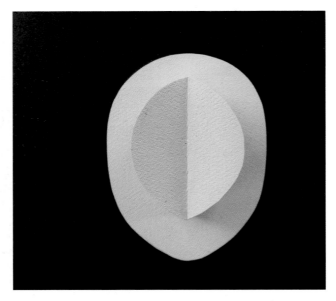

9. Once the hat is fully dry, trim away the excess paper.

10. Measure and cut an egg-shaped brim for the hat, then glue the top part of the hat to it.

11. Curl the sides of the hat up and curl the front down slightly. Add details if you wish.

GOLF CAP

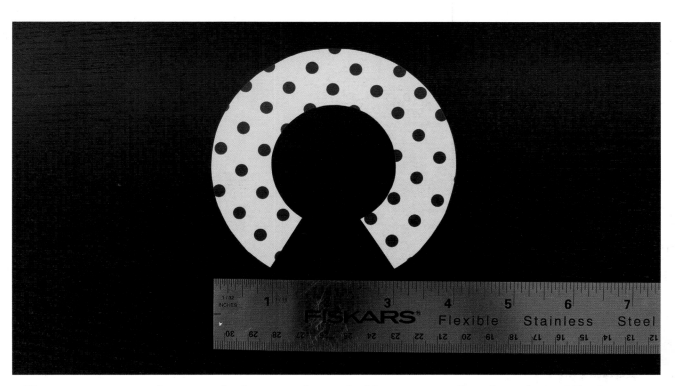

1. Use your compass to draw a circle about 4 inches wide. Measure a small circle in the middle about 2 inches wide. Cut the large circle out, then cut into the circle and cut the smaller circle out of the larger one. Now cut a chunk out of this ring shape you've made so you essentially have a C shape.

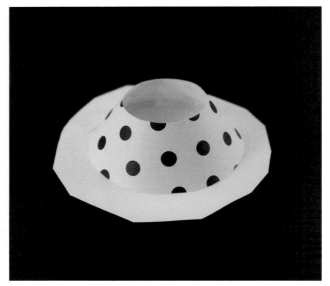

2. Measure this paper around into a sort of
   cropped cone shape, adjusting to find the size
   you want. Trim the excess, then glue the paper
   into the cone shape you've just measured.

3. Glue the wider side down to a piece of paper as
   shown. Trim the excess once dry.

4. Cut a strip of paper roughly ½ inch wide, glue it into a ring, and place it around the smaller opening of the hat. Apply glue to the inner seam.

5. Flip the hat over, add another, thinner band and a bow (preferably the same color, although the second band is optional), and glue a small pom-pom to the top. If you don't have a pom-pom, cotton balls and rolled-up tissues also work. If your cats shed a lot, you can use their old fur to roll a pom-pom.

GONDOLIER HAT

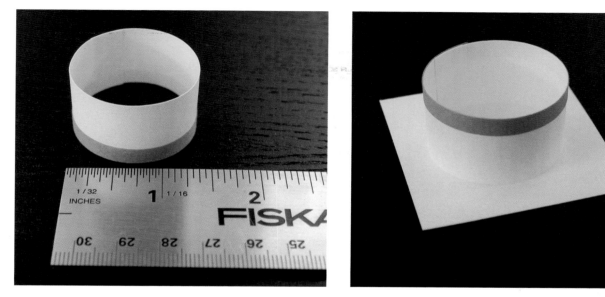

1. Cut a strip of paper about 4½ inches long and ¾ inch wide. Glue it into a short cylinder, and glue a thin strip around the base.

2. Flip the cylinder over and glue it to a square of paper.

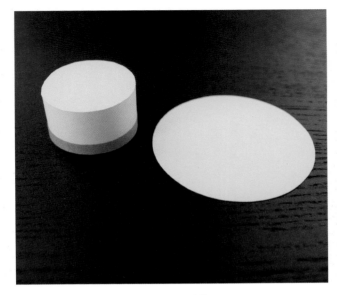

3. Once dry, trim the excess. Use your compass to draw and cut a circle. It should extend beyond the base of your hat by about ½ inch all around.

4. Glue this circle onto another piece of paper, preferably the same color as the band you added to the hat. Trim around the first circle, leaving a little bit of excess.

5. Glue the top of the hat onto the circular base.

6. Add some ribbons and a rose.

GRADUATION CAP

1. Cut a square of cardboard about
2 inches wide. Next, cut a square of
construction paper a little wider than
4 inches. Glue the cardboard square
to the middle of the paper square.

2. Use a ruler to measure and cut all the corners off the
paper. Make sure there is a little bit of excess paper
past each corner of the cardboard.

3. Fold and glue each triangular flap of paper over the cardboard. You might have to snip a little bit of construction paper off the corners of the hat.

4. Measure out and cut a cylinder. It can vary in size, but the diameter should be significantly smaller that the width of your square. Glue it to your square.

5. Flip the hat over and add a paper tassel. If you have string, that works, too.

HOLIDAY HAT

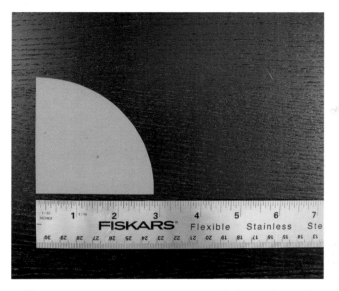

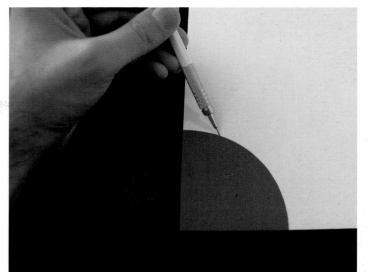

1. Use your compass to cut a curved shape from the corner of a piece of paper. It should be about 3 inches wide.

2. Using the piece you just cut as a template, line it up with the corner of another sheet of paper, preferably white (since this will be the trim of the hat). Trace the curve.

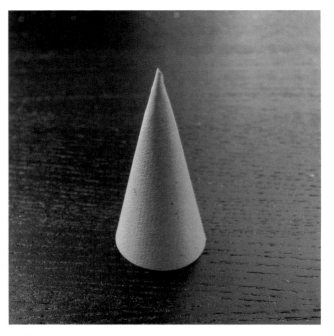

3. Cut along the line you just traced. Then use pattern scissors (or regular scissors, manually cutting a pattern as shown) to cut about ½ inch away from the first cut. You're only going to be using this middle strip, so discard the rest of the paper.

4. Fold and glue your original piece of paper into a cone.

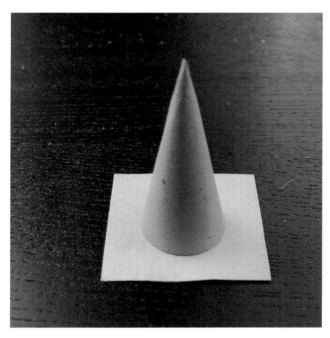

5. Glue the cone onto a small sheet of the same color paper.

6. Take the strip of patterned trim and curl it around the base of the cone, as shown. You'll need to measure the length first, mark it with a pen or pencil, then glue it into a ring. Now lower it down from the top of the cone.

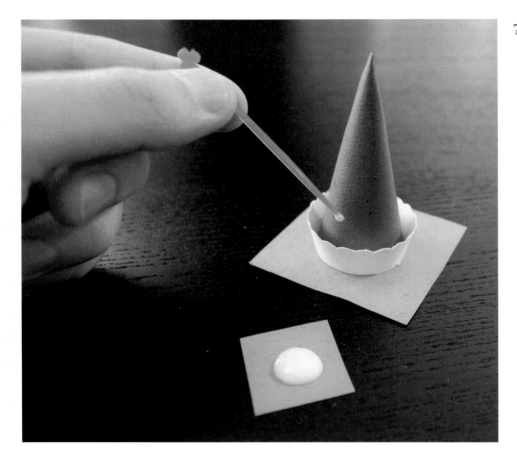

7. Use a toothpick to dab glue inside the ring of trim, just to make sure it seals snugly. You can also use a glue gun for this, but a toothpick makes it easier to reach the crevice.

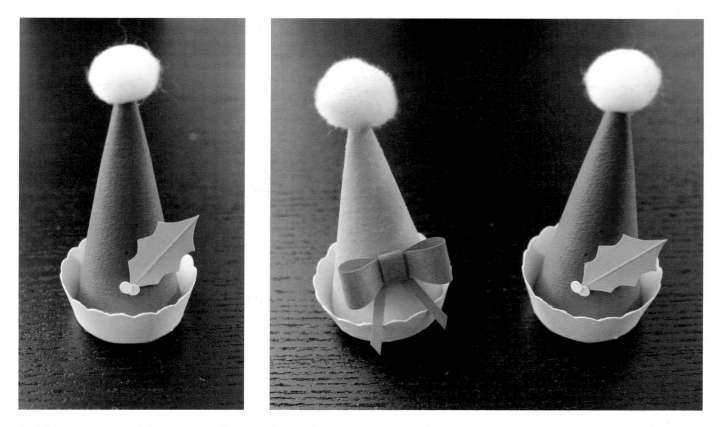

8. Add accessories, like leaves or bows. Glue a white pom-pom to the top with hot glue.

KNIGHT'S HELMET

1. Make a cylinder.

2. Cut two half-circle shapes. They should be roughly 2 inches long.

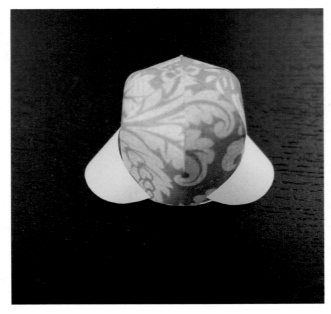 

3. Glue these half circles to the front and back of the hat. This is most easily done with your glue stick. Press the corners of each half circle against the hat until dry, then reinforce the inside with hot glue.

4. After fashioning these front and back brims, glue thin strips of paper over where they meet the dome. Glue the excess under the hat, or trim it if you wish.

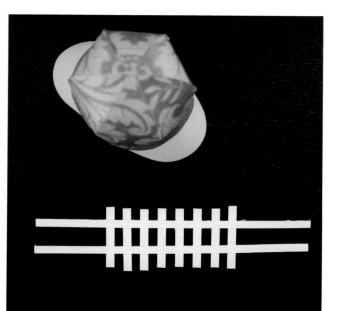

5. For the face guard, you're going to need several thin strips of paper. Cut two long strips, roughly 5 inches long, and 8 to 10 shorter strips, each roughly 1 inch or so in length.

6. Make a fence, essentially. With the longer strips parallel to each other and approximately ⅓ inch apart, glue the shorter strips between them. Sort of like railroad tracks, and the train is taking you to Craft City, USA.

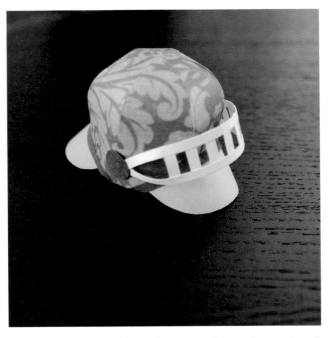

7. Trim the excess off the shorter strips, then glue the tips of the longer strips together. This should cause the face guard to naturally curve around, which you can adjust to your liking.

8. Glue each side of the face guard to either side of the hat, then add a small circle to each side as shown.

9. Add details. For this hat, I glued a small cylinder to the top, then inserted several small feathers with hot glue.

MAD HATTER HAT

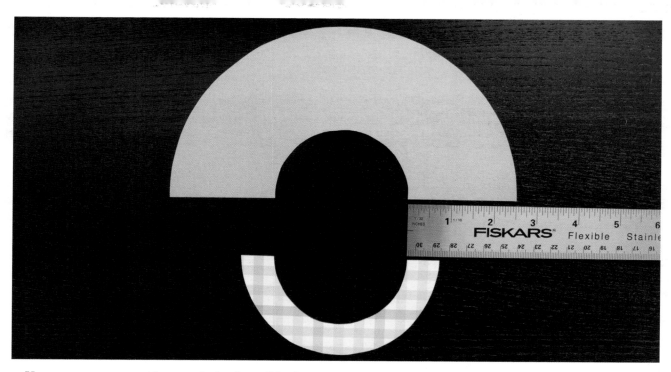

1. Use your compass to draw a circle about 3 inches wide (or 1½ inches from the center of your compass). From the same starting point, draw another circle about 8 inches wide (or 4 inches from the center). Cut out the larger circle, then cut the entire circle in half. Cut away the smaller half circle inside, so you have a large C shape.

For the smaller C shape, follow the same steps. Draw a 3-inch-wide circle, then adjust your compass to be slightly wider, and draw another circle around the first one. Cut it out the same way you cut the first shape.

2. Glue the smaller shape onto the larger shape as shown.

3. Glue the edges of this shape to create a cone.

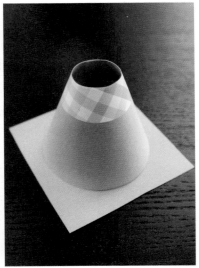

4. Glue the larger opening down onto a piece of paper.

5. Once the hat is dry, trim the excess paper. Glue the smaller opening onto a circle of paper as shown.

6. Add details, such as the Mad Hatter's trademark 10/6 card and a sewing pin (but snip off the sharp end with utility scissors first).

MARCHING BAND HAT

1. Start by making a cylinder. Adjust the width and height to your preference, but marching band hats should be fairly tall. Glue a thin band around the top and bottom.

2. Glue the cylinder down to a piece of paper the same color as your bands.

3. Once dry, trim the excess paper. Next, flip
   the hat over and glue it onto a piece of paper.
   This can be whatever color you choose. Leave
   enough on one side to cut a brim.

4. Once dry, trim the excess, leaving a half circle
   in front for the hat's brim.

5. Add a feather and a fancy emblem to the front of the hat.

MILITARY CAPTAIN HAT

1. Use your compass to draw a circle about 4 inches across. Adjust your compass about 1½ inches wider and, from the same center point, draw another circle. Cut out the larger circle, then cut the entire circle in half and cut out the smaller half circle that's left. You should now have a C shape.

2. Glue the ends of this C shape together, making a sort of cropped cone.

3. Glue the larger opening down onto a piece of paper of the same color or pattern.

4. Once dry, trim the excess. Next, cut a long strip of paper, roughly ¾ inch wide.

5. Curl the strip of paper into a cylinder shape and fit it around the smaller opening of your cone shape. The size will vary a bit. It shouldn't be so large that the tapered end of the cone extends beyond the cylinder shape. Once you've adjusted it to your liking, glue it around your cone shape as shown.

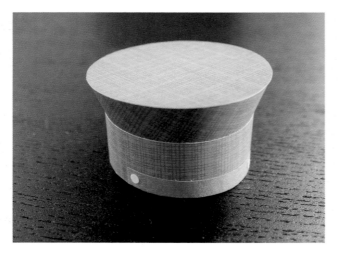

6. Flip the hat over and glue a small strip near the base. This strip should be a little less than 2 inches long. Use your hole punch to make tiny buttons, and glue them to each end of the strip.

7. Glue the entire hat down to a new piece of paper and trim the excess, leaving a circular shape for the brim.

8. To make the emblem for the hat, use a star-shaped hole punch to make a star, then glue it to a piece of yellow paper. If you don't have a star-shaped hole punch, you can draw a small black star with a pen.

9. Apply a glob of hot glue over the star shape and let the whole thing dry.

10. Trim around the glue, getting as close to the edge as possible. Cut out some small wing shapes, score them with your bone folder, and glue them to the back of the star emblem. Then glue this entire piece to the front of the hat.

PARTY HAT

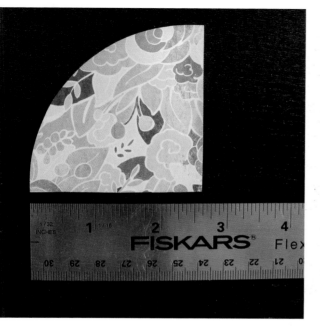

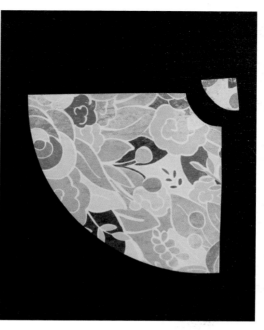

1. Using your compass, measure out about 3 inches from the corner of a piece of paper. Cut a quarter-circle shape.

2. Snip a curved bit off the tip of this triangular shape.

3. Curl and glue the paper into a cone shape, leaving a small opening at the top.

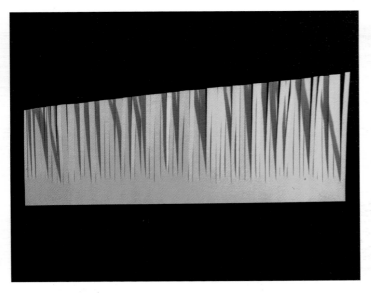

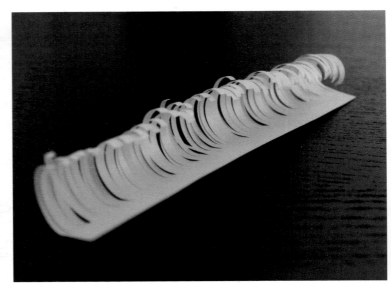

4. Cut a rectangular piece of paper with an angled top side. Five or 6 inches is a good length for this rectangle, but it can vary in size. Trim fringe along the angled top, stopping about ½ inch from the bottom.

5. Use your bone folder to curl the fringe. You can also use a pen for this.

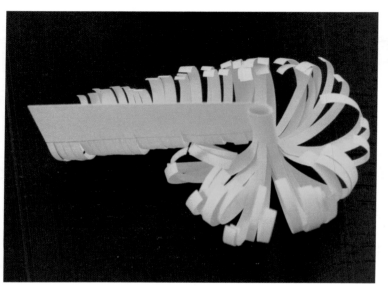

6. Starting from the end with the longest fringe, curl the strip inward and glue it when you reach the end.

7. Tuck this fringe piece into the top of your hat. If the opening isn't large enough, snip it little by little until it is.

PILGRIM
HAT

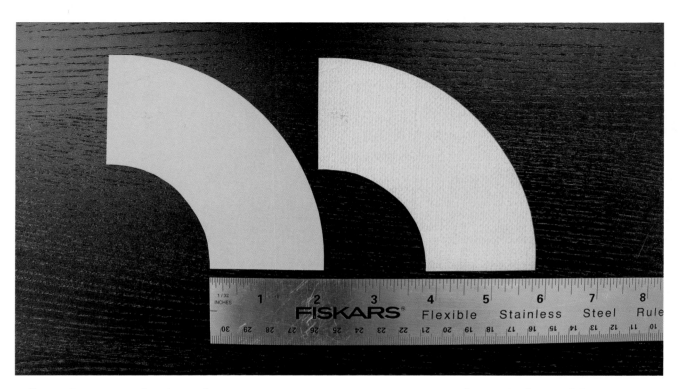

1. From the corner of a piece of paper, use your compass to measure out about 2 inches and draw a quarter circle across the paper. Then measure out about 4 inches from the same corner and draw another quarter circle. Cut out this curved strip. Repeat this process with a piece of paper of another color.

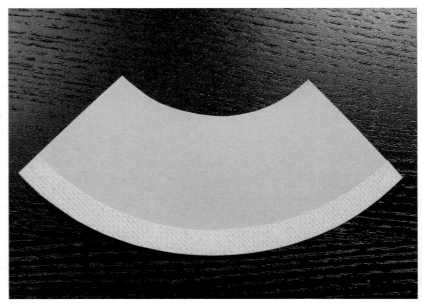

2. One of these strips is going to be used as trim.
   Cut a thin strip off the longer side.

3. Glue this thin strip to the corresponding side of your
   other piece of paper, lining it up as best you can.

4. Once the glue is dry, curl and glue this piece into a cone shape.

5. Glue the smaller opening onto a square of paper. Do this by dabbing the edge with a glue stick and then drizzling hot glue into the hat so the edges seal on the inside.

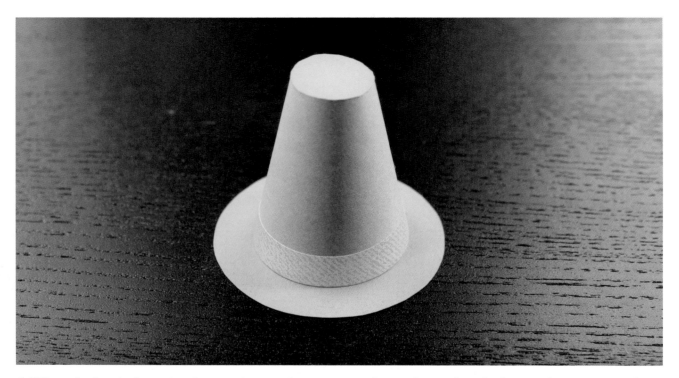

6. When the hat is dry, trim the excess away from the square piece. Flip the hat over and glue it onto a circular piece of paper. You can pre-cut the circle, or glue the hat to a larger piece of paper and trim once it's all dry.

7. Add accessories, like buckles, bows, and feathers.

PIRATE HAT

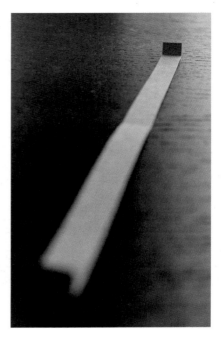

1. Cut two shapes similar to the image. They don't have to be exactly like the picture, but they should mirror each other. Either put two pieces of paper together, or cut one shape and use it as a template to cut another shape. Then cut a strip of paper that's twice as long as the base of each shape.

2. Fold the strip in half lengthwise, then fold up each corner slightly.

3. Glue the two folded flaps together, making sure they face inward.

4. Glue this oblong shape to a piece of paper.

5. Reinforce the inner seams with hot glue, and once it's dry trim the excess. Glue one of your hat shapes to the back of the oblong shape as shown.

6. Glue the other hat
shape to the other
side of the base,
doing your best to
get the hat shapes to
line up.

7. Add whatever trim and details you want.

POPE HAT

1. Cut two matching shapes as shown. They should resemble pointed arches and be roughly 3 inches wide, depending on how big your cat's head is. Glue crisscrossing strips across one of the shapes and trim the excess.

2. Glue the two pieces together into a cylindrical shape by having the edges of one shape overlap the other.

3. Add details and a fancy emblem. Have your kitty deliver a sermon to other neighborhood felines.

PRINCESS CONE

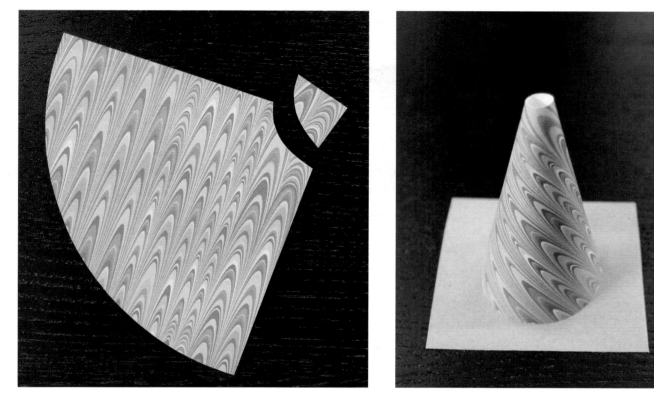

1. Follow the first 3 steps for making a Party Hat (page 139).

2. Glue the cone onto a sheet of paper.

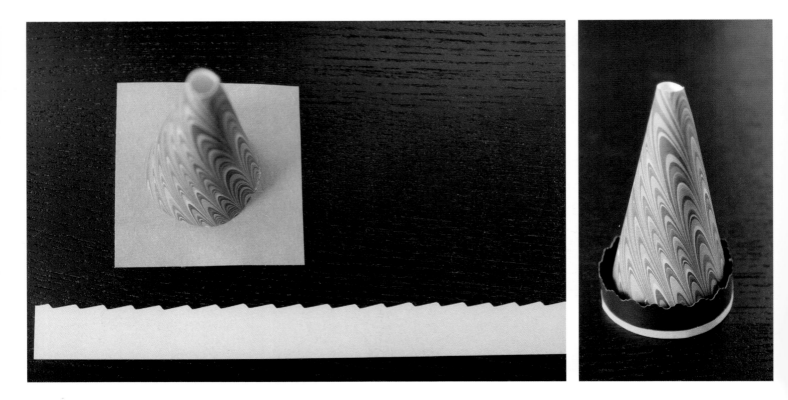

3. Cut a strip of paper, cutting patterns into one side. You can do this manually, but pattern scissors make life much easier. Measure and glue the strip around the base of your cone.

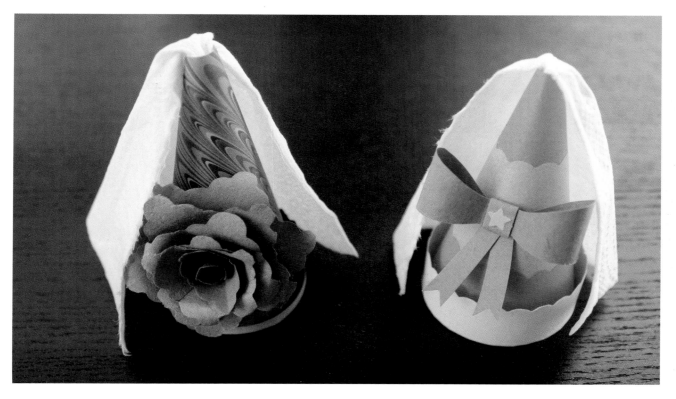

4. Stick a square of toilet paper into the top for a veil, or use tissue paper if you think you're too fancy for toilet paper. Add a flower or other details.

PROPELLER HAT

1. You're going to be making a dome, but it's a little different from typical domes. Use your template to cut out six different little arches, each from paper of a different color or pattern. Also cut a strip of paper that's longer than all your little arches lined up.

2. Line up and glue your arches onto the strip of paper, then continue with the usual directions for making a dome. Next, follow the directions on how to make a crown, and glue it around the base of your dome (page 91). This isn't completely necessary and you can continue on with just adding a propeller, but it's a nice detail to have.

3. For the propeller, you'll need a long strip of paper about ¾ inch wide, two long shapes for the actual propeller blade, and a small circle.

4. Roll up the strip until it's your desired thickness and glue it to the top of your hat. Glue the blades onto the rolled-up paper, then finish by gluing the little circle to the very top.

ROBIN HOOD HAT

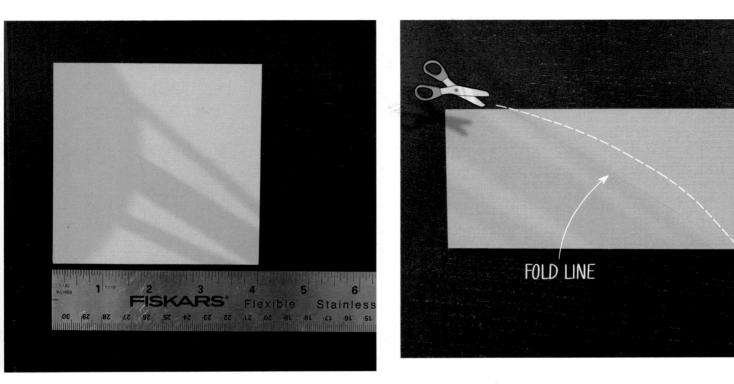

1. Cut a 4-inch square of paper.

2. Fold the paper in half. Use a ruler and your bone folder to score a line across the paper as shown.

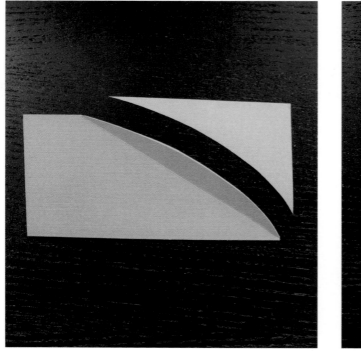

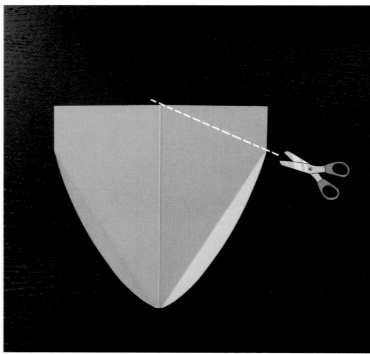

3. Cut a curved line across the top of the line you
   scored.

4. Unfold the paper, and snip off . . .

. . . one of the corners as shown.

5. Glue little crisscrossing strips across the center fold.

6. Fold the snipped corner over the corner you left intact and glue the hat together in the back.

7. Add a feather into the side of the hat.

SAFARI
HELMET

1. Start with the directions for making a dome, but use your hole punch to make a hole in each segment.

2. Continue making a dome.

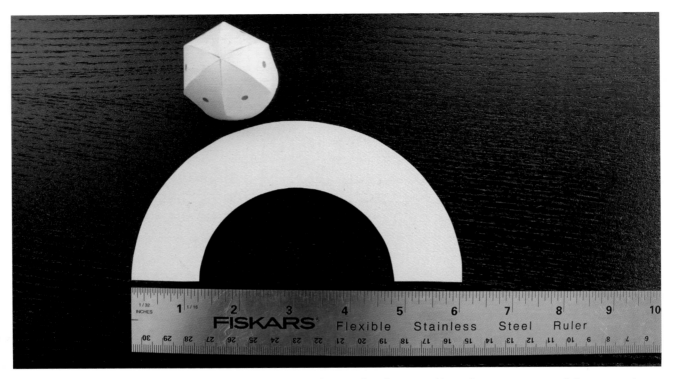

3. Use your compass to draw a circle about 4½ inches wide, then readjust the compass and draw another circle roughly 1½ inches beyond the first one. Cut out the larger circle, then cut the whole thing in half. Lastly, cut out the remaining half circle in the middle, so you have a curved strip as shown.

4. Curve this strip around into a cone shape, and measure out the smaller opening to fit around your dome. Mark the inside, trim, and glue.

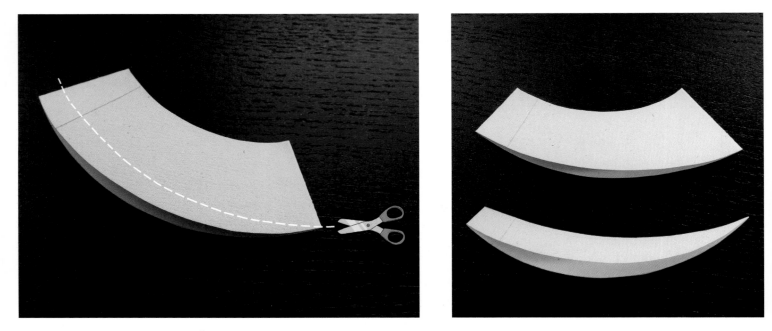

5. Once the glue is dry, flatten this cone as shown and make a curved cut along the base.

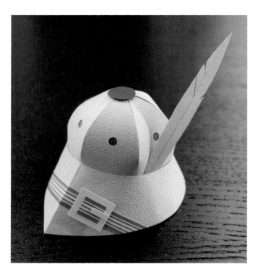

6. Open the trimmed cone shape back up and gently wedge the dome into it. About an inch of the dome should still be visible. Use hot glue on the inside to make sure the two pieces stick together.

7. Glue a strip across the front of the brim. Either trim the excess or glue it under the hat. Cut a small circle and glue it to the top of the hat.

8. Add a little belt buckle shape and a flower or feather. Send your kitty into the wilderness to explore.

SAILOR HAT

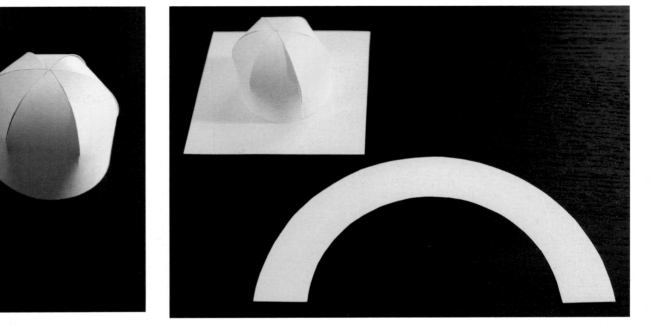

1. Make a dome.

2. Glue the dome onto a piece of paper. Next, use your compass to draw a circle about 4½ inches wide, then readjust the compass and draw another circle roughly 1 inch beyond the first. Cut out the larger circle, then cut the whole thing in half. Finally, cut out the remaining half circle in the middle, so you have a curved strip as shown.

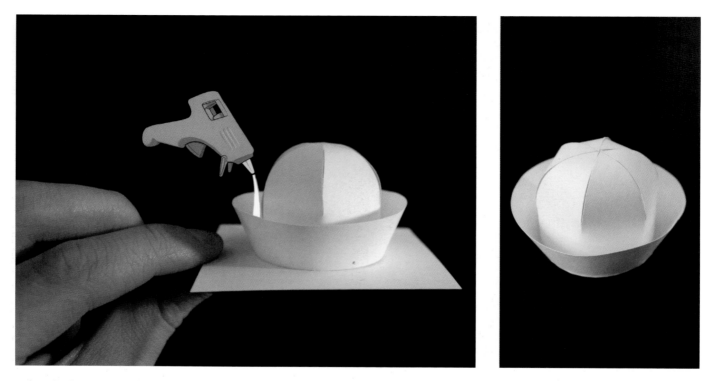

3. Curve this strip around into a cone shape, and measure out the smaller opening to fit around your dome. Mark the inside, trim, and glue it together. Then glue this piece around the base of your dome as shown. Trim the excess.

4. Add whatever details you wish.

SAMURAI HELMET
(KABUTO)

1. Make a dome, then glue thin strips of paper over the seams.

2. Cut two half-circle shapes as shown, one larger than the other. Measurements don't have to be exact, but the larger one should be about 3½ inches long, and the other about 2½ inches.

3. Glue these half circles to the front and back of the hat. This is most easily done with your glue stick. Press the corners of each half circle against the hat until dry, then reinforce the underside with hot glue.

4. Glue thin strips over the seam of the front and back brims and either trim the excess or glue it under the hat.

5. Cut two strips of paper like the one shown. Each should be about 2½ inches long and a little under 1 inch wide.

6. Curl the strips with your bone folder and glue one to each side of your helmet, as shown, by folding one end of the strip and gluing it to the inside of the hat.

7. For the crest, fold a piece of paper, and draw a shape resembling the one shown.

8. Cut out the shape and glue it to the front of your helmet.

9. Cut out a decorative emblem and glue it to the front of the crest. You can decide to be finished now, or you can go the extra mile and glue a tiny origami animal to the top of your helmet. I chose a crane; you can find directions for this and about a million other animals online.

SANDWICH HAT

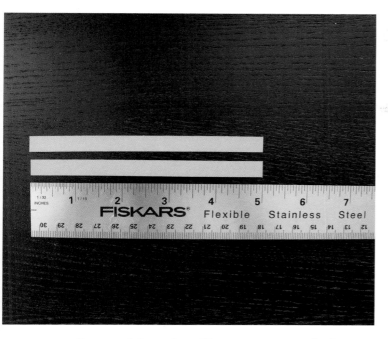

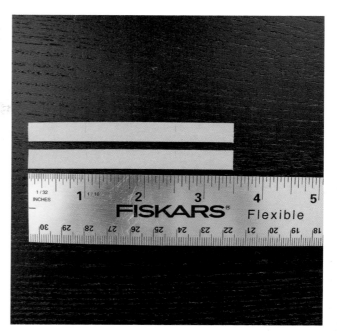

1. Cut two thin strips of brown paper, each about 5 inches long. They should be roughly ⅓ inch wide.

2. Cut two more strips of the same brown paper and of the same width, this time measuring three separate lengths and marking them on the paper: first 1 inch, then 1½ inches, then another inch.

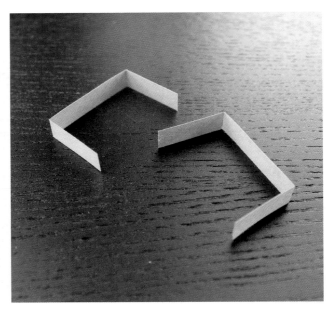

3. Take one of the longer strips, glue it into a ring, and then glue it to a piece of pale yellow or light brown paper, making sure it's oblong and not a perfect circle. Reinforce the inner seams with hot glue. Repeat this process with the second longer strip.

4. Fold the smaller brown strips at the marks you measured, making large bracket shapes.

5. Glue one of these bracket shapes underneath each oblong circle, as shown.

6. Once the glue is dry, trim the excess paper, then flip the piece over and glue it to another piece of paper.

7. Trim the excess, and repeat to make two "bread" pieces in total. Don't eat them, as delicious as they look.

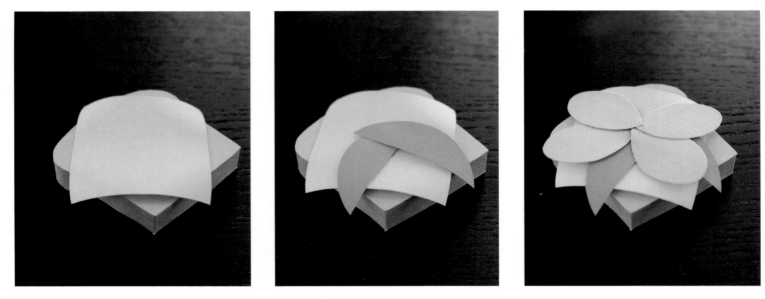

8. Stack "ingredients" onto one slice of bread: yellow squares for cheese, orange or red half circles for tomatoes, green leaves of spinach or lettuce, and so on.

9. Glue the second bread piece on top, then snip a sandwich toothpick in half and
glue it in the very center.

SERVICE HAT

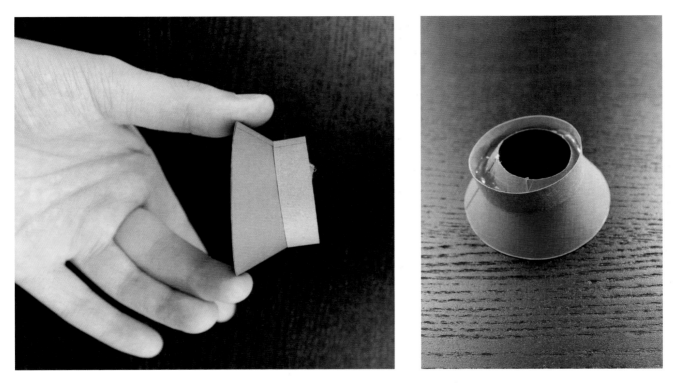

1. Follow steps 1–4 for the making the Golf Cap (page 100).

2. Glue the hat down to a piece of paper, then trim the excess, leaving a curved brim in the front (the front being the highest part of the hat).

3. Add some sort of emblem to the hat. I decided this was a mailman's hat, but you can add police, firefighter, or milkman emblems. Be creative!

SHERLOCK HAT

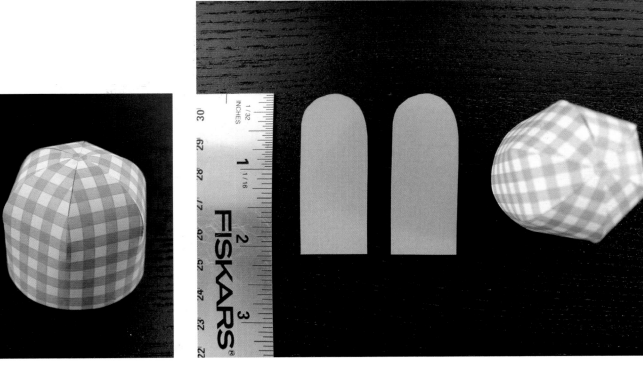

1. Make a dome.

2. Cut two strips of paper with rounded edges. These should be the width of your dome template and about 2 inches long, depending on how big your dome template is.

3. Glue these strips, rounded sides pointing up, to the sides of your hat.

4. Glue the tops of these strips to the top of your hat.

5. Glue the entire hat onto a long strip of paper.

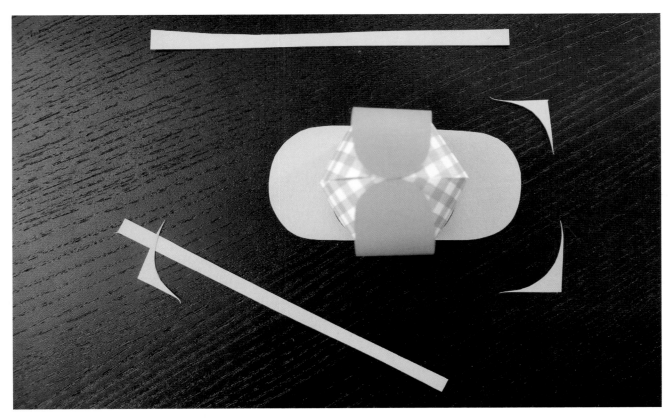

6. Trim the excess away, leaving a front and back brim as shown.

7. Curl up the edge of each brim, and glue a thin strip of paper to the top of the hat.

8. Add a bow to the top of the hat, right in the center of the tiny strip you glued down.

SNAPBACK

1. Start by cutting a pattern for a dome.

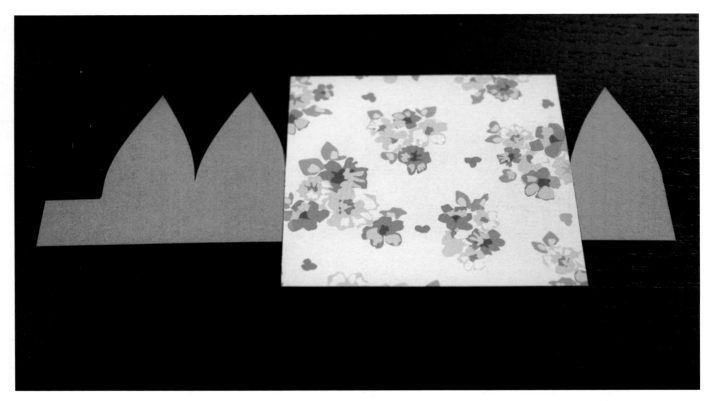

2. Measure a piece of decorative paper just wide enough to cover three arches of the dome pattern, and glue it over them.

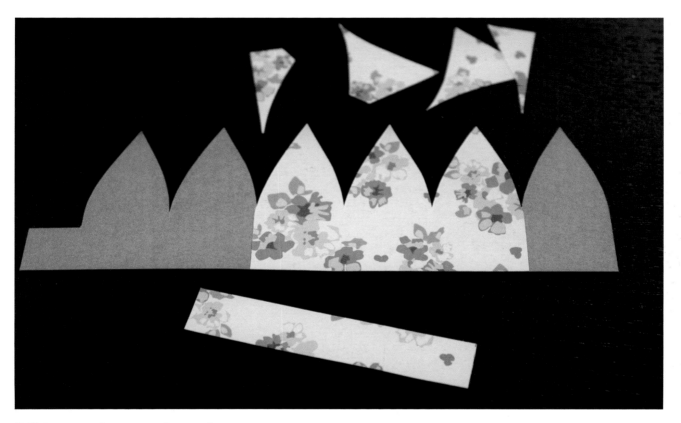

3. Trim away the excess decorative paper.

4. Finish making the dome. Add a small circle to the top of the hat, then glue the whole thing onto
   another piece of paper as shown.

5. Trace the shape of a bill on the base piece of paper. Trim away the excess, leaving a rounded brim in front of the hat (the side with the decorative paper).

SUMMER HAT

1. Make a dome.

2. Glue a thin band around the base of your hat, then use your compass to cut out a circle that's at least ½ inch larger on all sides than your dome.

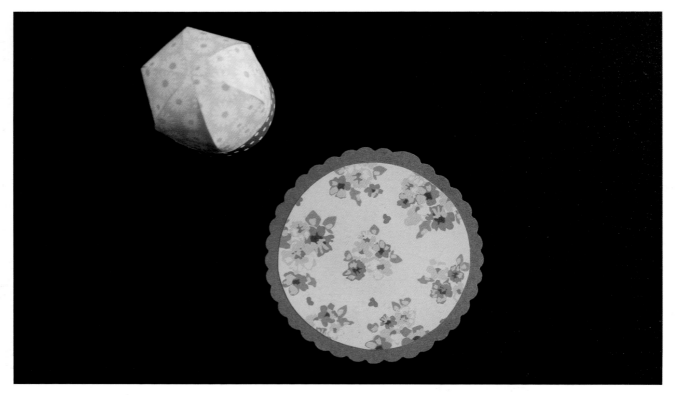

3. Glue the circle onto another piece of paper, then trim around the outside with pattern-making scissors. If you don't have pattern scissors, you can use regular scissors to cut an interesting edge.

4. Glue the dome onto the circular piece, and add details like flowers and bows.

TAM-O-SHANTER

1. Use your compass to draw a circle about 2 inches wide. Then use your dome template piece to trace out eight "petals" from the very center of the circle. This doesn't have to be exact, but the petal shapes should be long enough to curve around and touch the center of the circle.

2. With your bone folder, curl the
   petal shapes inward.

3. Glue every other petal to the center of the hat
   as shown.

4. Once this is dry, glue the
   remaining petals to
   the center.

5. Glue a small pom-pom to the center of the hat.

TOP HAT

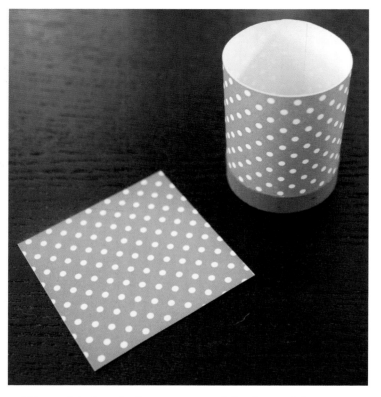

1. Make a cylinder. Experiment with size, since top hats can be short or very tall.

2. Glue a thin band of paper around the base of the cylinder, then cut a square of paper that's about twice as wide as the base of your hat.

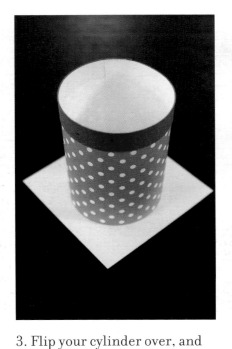

3. Flip your cylinder over, and glue it to the back side of the square you just cut.

4. Once the glue is dry, trim the excess paper.

5. Flip the hat over again, and glue it to a circle of construction paper.

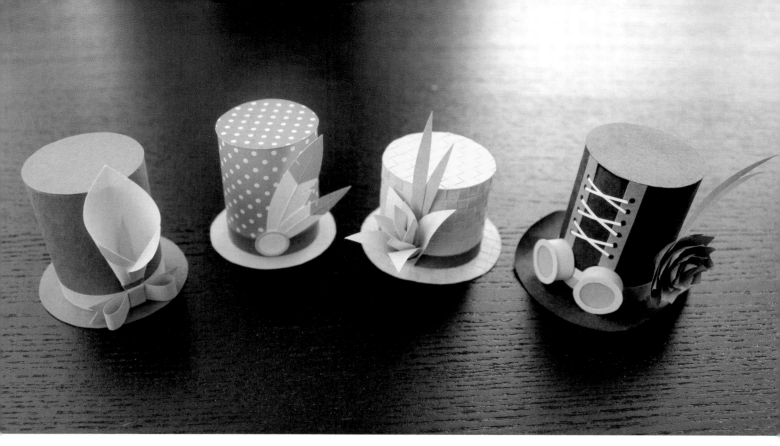

6. Add details like feathers, bows, and flowers.

TRICORN

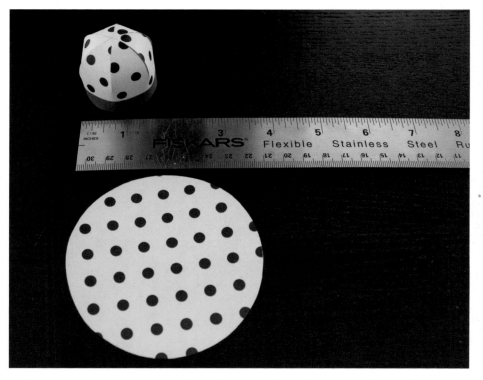

1. Make a dome and glue a thin band of paper around the base.

2. Use your compass to cut a fairly large circle—about 4 inches wide. You'll be curling the edges of this circle, so you might want to glue it to another circle of a different color for some visual interest.

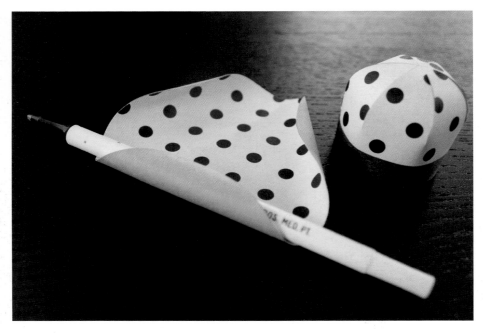

3. Use a pen to curl up three edges of this circle. This will most likely involve some trial and error, but you want three equal points once you're done.

4. Glue the dome into the center of the circular piece. If you want, you can hot-glue the curled part of the brim to the dome for added sturdiness.

5. Add a buckle to the front of the hat, and any other details you wish.

VALKYRIE HAT

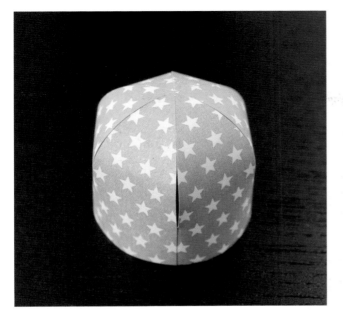

1. Make a dome.

2. Glue thin strips of paper over the seams of the dome, then glue a thin band of paper around the base of the hat.

3. Glue a small cone to the top of the hat. The wings are much easier than they may appear:
   Simply make three or four feathers and glue them together in a fan shape. Then cut
   a smaller winged shape like the one you see in the photo, and glue it over the fanned
   feathers. Finally, glue it to the side of the hat, then glue a circular shape over that.
   You can get creative if you want and give the hat bat wings. Do this by cutting bat wing
   shapes out of a single piece of paper.

WITCH HAT

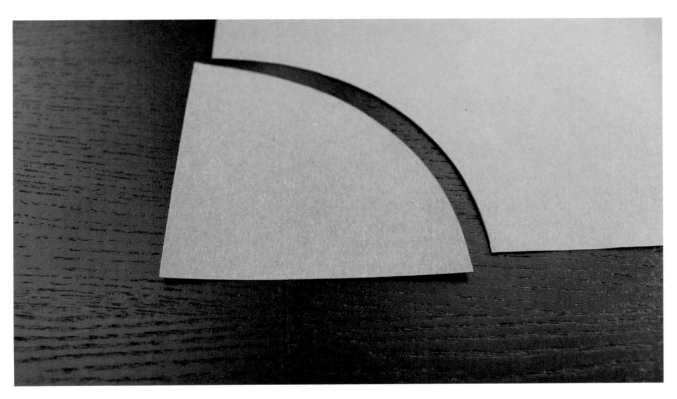

1. Use your compass to measure about 3 inches out from the corner of a piece of paper.
   Cut out this triangular piece.

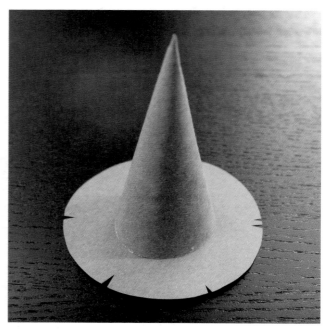

2. Glue the piece into a cone shape.

3. Glue the cone to the center of a circle. Snip little pieces out of the circle.

4. Cut a strip of paper only about ¼ inch wide. Measure the length around the base of the cone, mark it with your pen or pencil, and glue it into a ring shape. Dab one edge of the ring with your glue stick, then press it down around the base of the cone.

5. Add a buckle to the front of the hat, and add whatever details you wish. Make sure your cat knows it should only use magic for good, not evil.

ACKNOWLEDGMENTS

I WANT TO THANK all the cats who modeled for this book, and their owners for letting me intrude in their homes and put hats on their animals. Thanks to my agent Monika Verma and my editor Morgan Hedden for guiding me through the tricky process of making a craft book. Thanks to my local Michaels for having killer sales on construction paper, and thank you to Martha Stewart for making my favorite kind of glue sticks. They're somehow just better than other glue sticks.

ABOUT THE CATS

NAME: MAXWELL

APPROXIMATE AGE: Just turned 2

BREED: Anyone's guess!

FAVORITE FOOD OR TREAT: Sardines in lobster consommé

FAVORITE PLACE TO SLEEP: On the top bunk of a bunk bed made for American Girl dolls

Maxwell is an amputee due to a mysterious paralyzed leg he had as a baby. Even though he's a tripod he gets around fine and is actually incredibly lazy and spoiled.

NAME: PEPPERCORN

APPROXIMATE AGE: 2

BREED: American shorthair, most likely

FAVORITE FOOD OR TREAT: Little bits of cream cheese off your morning bagel

FAVORITE PLACE TO SLEEP: Any cardboard box she can find

Pepper's shelter waived her adoption fee because she wouldn't stop biting people who tried to pet her. She doesn't bite anymore. Usually.

NAME: FITZ

APPROXIMATE AGE: 2

BREED: Half Russian Blue, half unkown

FAVORITE FOOD OR TREAT: Prosciutto

FAVORITE PLACE TO SLEEP: On her human's legs

Should note that she was born in Russia and is a proud emigrant to NY! She is very talkative and if she spoke human she would definitely be voiced by a Russian James Bond villainess.

NAME: COLONEL MUSTARD

APPROXIMATE AGE: 5

BREED: Maine Coon

FAVORITE FOOD OR TREAT: He's obsessed with cat grass. He makes crazy noises every morning until it's taken off the shelf and he gets some.

FAVORITE PLACE TO SLEEP: On top of you while you're sleeping

The Colonel is a very dog-like cat. He loves affection and friends, and is basically Garfield come to life.

NAME: BENNY

APPROXIMATE AGE: 10

BREED: Maine Coon mix, possibly. He was a stray!

FAVORITE FOOD OR TREAT: Hickory Smoked Tofurky slices (Seriously—he can smell it from three rooms away.)

FAVORITE PLACE TO SLEEP: Your suitcase

Benny is the strangest cat I've ever met. When I first adopted him, in 2007, he used to try to drink my coffee and also had a thing for Hawaiian Punch. (He's since outgrown his taste for both.) He was also really into hanging out on my bathtub ledge and peeking in to surprise me when I was taking a shower. Also, when he would do something bad and I'd spray him with water, instead of running away, he'd open his mouth and catch/drink the water. I don't know who raised this cat.

NAME: INGA FURLAN-FATATO

APPROXIMATE AGE: About 4

BREED: Domestic shorthair/former Prospect Park street hustler

FAVORITE FOOD OR TREAT: Tortilla chips

FAVORITE PLACE TO SLEEP: On the back of the couch, inhaling the heat from the radiator like a weird cat drug addict

Inga is a beauty queen and is very dedicated to fashion and grooming.

ABOUT THE AUTHOR

ADAM ELLIS is a twenty-nine-year-old artist and blogger and works as an illustrator at BuzzFeed. His first book, *Books of Adam: The Blunder Years*, was published by Grand Central Publishing in 2013. Originally from Montana, Adam now lives in New York City with his two cats, Maxwell and Peppercorn.